spot

CREEPY CRAWLIES

ANTS

by Nessa Black

AMICUS | AMICUS INK

legs

antennas

Look for these
words and pictures
as you read.

jaws

anthill

Have you ever seen an ant work?

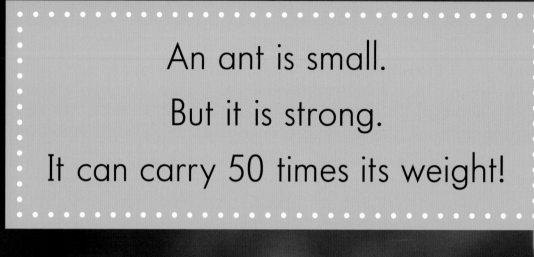

An ant is small.

But it is strong.

It can carry 50 times its weight!

legs

Do you see its legs?

An ant has six legs.

They are very thin.

antennas

Do you see its antennas?
They help the ant find food.
They smell, touch, and taste.

Do you see its jaws?
They are strong and sharp.
They cut leaves.
They carry food.

jaws

anthill

Do you see the anthill?
There is a big home under it.
It has many tunnels.

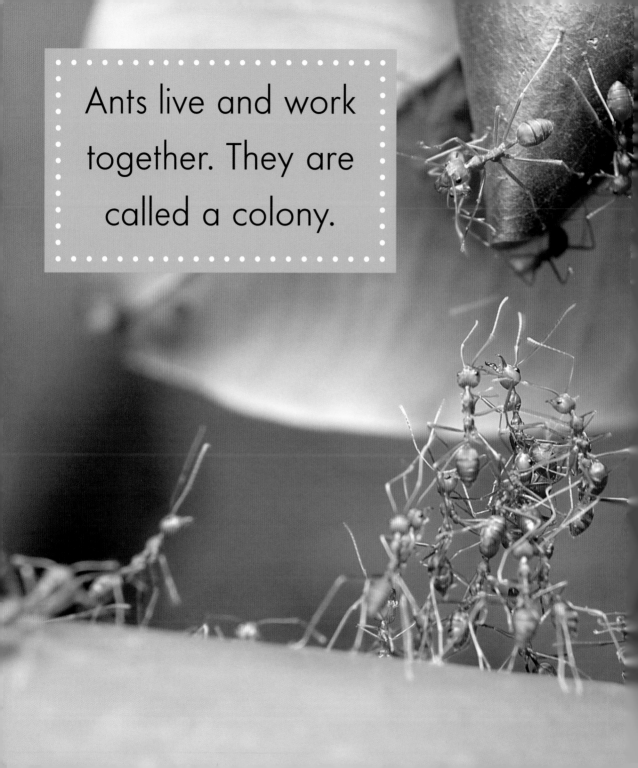

Ants live and work together. They are called a colony.

legs

Do you see its legs?
An ant has six legs.
They are very thin.

legs

antennas

Do you see its antennas?
They help the ant find food.
They smell, touch, and taste.

antennas

Did you find?

jaws

anthill

Do you see its jaws?
They are strong and sharp.
They cut leaves.
They carry food.

jaws

anthill

Do you see the anthill?
There is a big home under it.
It has many tunnels.

Spot is published by Amicus and Amicus Ink
P.O. Box 1329, Mankato, MN 56002
www.amicuspublishing.us

Library of Congress Cataloging-in-Publication Data
Names: Black, Nessa, author.
Title: Ants / by Nessa Black.
Description: Mankato, Minnesota : Amicus, [2018] | Series:
  Spot. Creepy crawlies | Audience: K to grade 3.
Identifiers: LCCN 2016055565 (print) | LCCN 2016059933
  (ebook) | ISBN 9781681511047 (library binding) | ISBN
  9781681522234 (pbk.) | ISBN 9781681511948 (e-book)
Subjects: LCSH: Ants--Juvenile literature.
Classification: LCC QL568.F7 B567 2018 (print) | LCC
  QL568.F7 (ebook) | DDC 595.79/6--dc23
LC record available at https://lccn.loc.gov/2016055565

Printed in China

HC 10 9 8 7 6 5 4 3 2 1
PB 10 9 8 7 6 5 4 3 2 1

Wendy Dieker, editor
Deb Miner, series designer
Ciara Beitlich, book designer
Holly Young, photo researcher

Photos by iStock cover, 3, 8–9, 14–15;
Shutterstock 1, 6–7, 10–11, 12–13;
Superstock 4–5

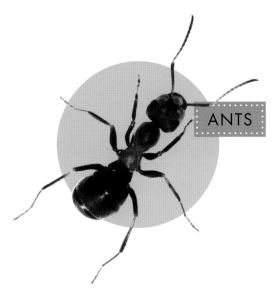

ANTS